A typical Icelandic Pony, with a
refined, elongated head, bright eyes
and short, mouse-like ears. The long
mane and thick forelock are
distinctive features of the Icelandic.

In 874 AD a group of Norwegian farmers of Viking origin left their homeland and sailed towards the island of Iceland. They had had a dispute with King Harald Fairhair who was trying to force them to submit to his rule. But the proud Vikings were used to their freedom and would not capitulate. Therefore, they decided to leave their homes and settle in the uninhabited island of Iceland, which they had discovered in the course of their war expeditions across the North Sea. As well as their wives, children, servants and cattle, they also took with them their horses, which were of the small, stocky, Germanic type. Other horses were then brought to Iceland by these settlers from the coast of Ireland and Scotland, which they plundered in various raids at that time. These horses were of Celtic origin and were lighter and more refined than the Germanic ponies. Both these groups of horses formed the basis for the horses which have been bred for over a thousand years in Iceland and which are called Icelandic Ponies.

Iceland is hardly a paradise for horses. The climate is bitterly cold and the land is bleak. The Icelandic Ponies, which lived for centuries in semi-wild herds, neglected by the people who lived alongside them, have had to overcome an extremely hostile environment with thick snow and icy storms. However it was this environment which caused the Icelandic Ponies to develop their extraordinary hardiness and undemanding nature. Innumerable herds of Icelandic Ponies were wiped out by natural catastrophes. Of the 35,000 or so horses which were present on the island in 1780, only about 8,400 survived an enormous volcanic eruption in 1783. However soon after that, in 1804, there were once more about 26,000 horses in Iceland. Today the estimated number of Icelandic Ponies in their native island is around 60,000. Most of them graze in semi-wild herds in inaccessible highlands and steep valleys. For hundreds of years the population of Iceland has been a population of horsemen. In the capital, Rekjavik, there are many riding stables accommodating about 1,000 horses.

ICEL~~~~~~NIES

SUNBURST BOOKS

*Icelandic Ponies in their element, running wild in the herd
through the wind and rain.*

Although Iceland's horses have been pure-bred for about 1,000 years, the horses in different areas of Iceland have their own distinctive characteristics. In north Iceland, around Skagafjördur, one of the most famous breeding areas in the country, the horses have slender limbs and are very docile and responsive. The horses in the south of the island in the area of Hornafjördur are somewhat larger and tougher, but lack the smooth gait which is so highly valued by recreational riders.

The herd of the St. Margarethe Icelandic Pony Centre in Bavaria, at full gallop across the meadow.

The goal of Icelandic Pony breeders, both in Iceland and in secondary breeding areas, is to produce a robust, placid horse with a smooth gait. Perfomance is more important to the breeders than appearance. This is demonstrated in the marks awarded when the horses are judged: 60% of the marks are allotted to riding quality and only 40% to build and appearance.

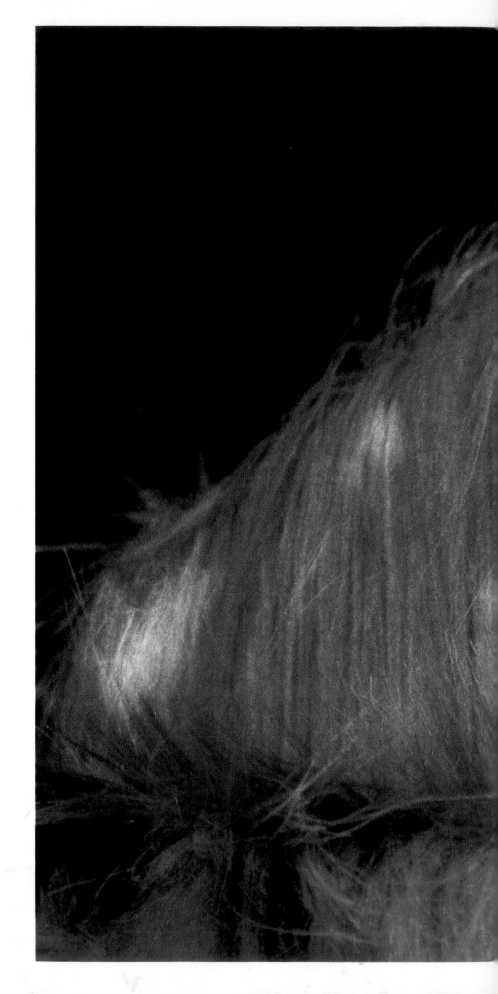

The Roudblessot Hestar line - chestnut with white points - has long been acknowledged as the best riding horse in Iceland.

The most important season for horse breeders is the summer, when the Icelandic Ponies give birth to their foals, and the breeder can see whether he has chosen the right stallion for his mares.

*This small foal, only a few days old, stands rather unsteadily on his legs,
staying close to his mother for protection.*

These two slightly older foals have already built up a friendship with each other.
(Photo: Elisabeth Kellner)

The foals always return to their mothers for a drink of milk.

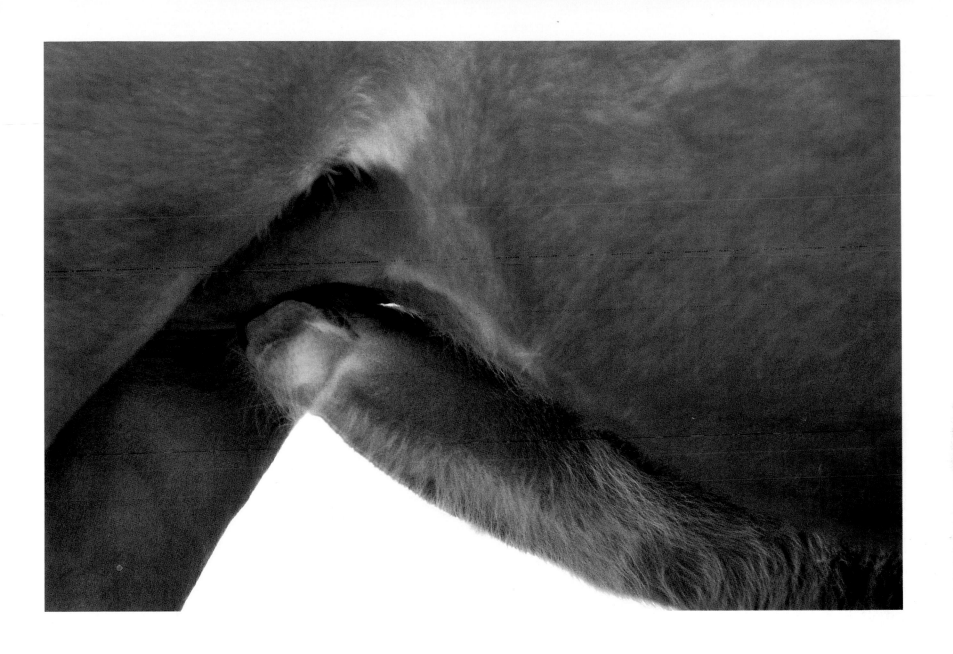

The foals stay with their mothers for about 6 months before they are separated and divided into herds of colts and fillies.

But that's a long way off for this foal.
He still has the whole summer to
spend with his mother grazing in the
green meadows.

The foals begin to eat grass and herbs quite early on. But this little piebald is still too young and prefers his mother's milk.

*Geldings from the Vomperberg Riding School in
the mountain meadows of the Tyrol.*

A mock fight between two geldings. In a herd horses constantly stage these playful confrontations, challenging the existing hierarchy and asserting their strength.

This is also a playful challenge: through gentle nips with his teeth this dun colt tries to provoke the others to engage in a mock fight.

The most distinctive feature of the Icelandic Pony is its gait. A true Icelandic Pony does not only move at a walk, trot, canter or gallop - it also uses two other gaits: the "tilt" and the "pace." The only other breeds which have the ability to use these gaits are the Peruvian Paso and the American Saddle Horse. Like the walk, the tilt is a four-beat gait and it also has the same foot pattern: left hind, left fore, right hind, right fore. However, whereas at a walk the horse always has two or three hooves on the ground at any given time, in the tilt there are only one or two hooves on the ground at a time. The pace is a two-beat action. The legs on either side work in tandem: left hind and left fore together and right hind and right fore together. The pace is defined as a racing gait. In order not to overtax the horses, pace races are restricted to distances between 150 and 250 metres.

As autumn closes in the horses already have their thick winter coats, but still prefer to be out in the open rather than in their shelters.

*Icelandic Ponies have an impressive, silky mane which is usually divided,
falling on both sides of the neck.*

Skin care Icelandic style: this young stallion from the Hausruckhof Stud rolls to scratch his back in those places which he can't reach with his teeth and hooves.

Every colour of coat can be found amongst Icelandic Ponies. The most common colours are chestnut, bay and black, as well as, to a lesser extent, grey.

This grey gelding appears to be one of the most high-ranking horses in the herd hierarchy. With his teeth bared, he tries to stop the other horses from overtaking him.

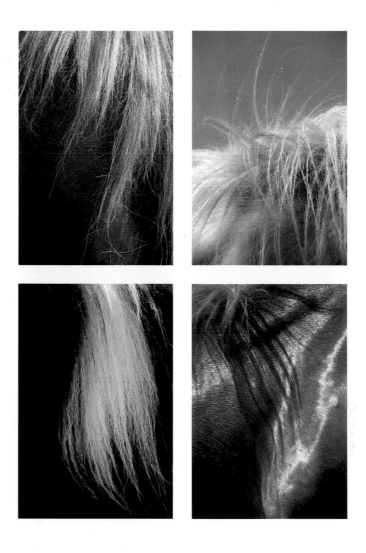

The many different colours of manes
of the Icelandic Ponies.

Icelandic Ponies aren't suited to being kept in warm, closed stables. It would be torture for them to wait there all day until their owner came to set them free from the boredom of doing nothing. They feel best in a herd, which is what they have been used to for hundreds of years in their homeland. Ideally they should be kept in a herd out in the open with access to a stall for shelter. That way they are free to decide where they want to be. They will usually only make use of the stall when it is raining, or in summer when the sun is too strong and they're plagued by flies. Even in the snow they love to race around. Their coats are so thick that the snow does not penetrate them.

Grey horses in the fog ...... Even when the weather is cold and damp the Icelandic Ponies prefer to be out in the open.

Portrait of a liver chestnut gelding with
white mane from the Hausruckhof Stud.

From spring through to autumn grass is the basic food for robust animals like the Icelandic Ponies. They only require concentrated feed if high demands are being made of them. In winter hay will suffice.

The herd of young stallions at the Hausruckhof Stud. It is only when they are four years old that the horses gradually get used to people, when they are broken in and put forward for stud work.

Most of these young stallions will earn their keep as riding horses. Only a few will be privileged enough to be registered as stud stallions and make their contribution towards the breeding of Icelandic Ponies in Austria.

Prior to the middle of the 19th century, virtually no horses from Iceland had been seen elsewhere in Europe. The first major exportation of these horses took place in about 1850, when coal mine managers in England realised that the small, tough Icelandic Ponies would make ideal pit ponies to pull the coal wagons in the depths of the mines. It wasn't until a hundred years later, in 1950, that Icelandic Ponies were first imported into Germany, but before long these small horses from the cold, northern island had won many friends throughout Europe. In 1970 an international association, the European Federation of Friends of the Icelandic Pony was formed, and this organisation now has over 25,000 Icelandic Ponies registered outside of Iceland.

Icelandic Ponies are in their element in the snow. They rush around happily in the white carpeted meadows.

Within a relatively short time, the Icelandic Pony has won a huge following throughout Europe. It is an ideal horse for the recreational rider: characterful but calm, tough and hard-working, foot-sure and plucky. The ambling tilt gait of the Icelandic makes riding much more pleasurable for older people or those with back problems. On cross-country rides the Icelandic is in its element, covering 40 or 50 kilometres a day without problems. Icelandic Ponies really enjoy outings in large groups and very rarely fight among themselves along the way. Those who are more interested in competitive sports also achieve great success with these fast, agile horses.

Some of the Roudblessot Hestar line of Icelandics - galloping through the snow in the fading light of the winter sun.

A stallion fight in the snow. Almost lying in the deep snow, these two grey stallions are trying to bite each other's forelegs. The Icelandic stallions are renowned for their spirit. Up until the 16th century stallion fights were held regularly in Iceland. But the stallions were very rarely injured badly, as their owners would separate them before it got to that stage.

Rearing up on the hind legs is also part of the ritual of stallion fights. From this position the stallion can inflict hefty blows on his opponent's chest with his forelegs.

This young stallion flares his nostrils in response to an interesting smell which he has detected in the air.